W9-BLK-084

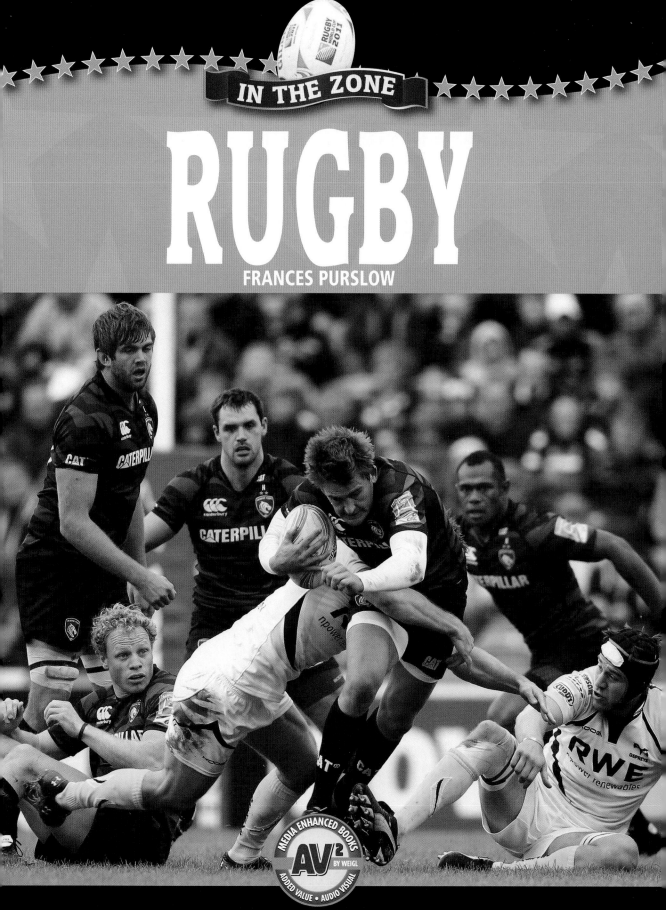

IN THE ZONE

RUGBY

FRANCES PURSLOW

AV²
BY WEIGL
MEDIA ENHANCED BOOKS
ADDED VALUE • AUDIO VISUAL

www.av2books.com

Go to **www.av2books.com,**
and enter this book's
unique code.

BOOK CODE

S 2 5 1 5 3 4

AV² by Weigl brings you
media enhanced books that
support active learning.

Download the AV² catalog at
www.av2books.com/catalog

AV² provides enriched content that supplements and complements this book.
Weigl's AV² books strive to create inspired learning and engage young minds
in a total learning experience.

Your AV² Media Enhanced books come alive with...

Audio
Listen to sections of
the book read aloud.

Key Words
Study vocabulary, and
complete a matching
word activity.

Video
Watch informative
video clips.

Quizzes
Test your knowledge.

Embedded Weblinks
Gain additional information
for research.

Slide Show
View images and
captions, and prepare
a presentation.

Try This!
Complete activities and
hands-on experiments.

... and much, much more!

AV² Online Navigation on page 24

Published by AV² by Weigl
350 5th Avenue, 59th Floor
New York, NY 10118
Website: www.av2books.com   www.weigl.com

Library of Congress Cataloging-in-Publication Data
Purslow, Frances.
Rugby / Frances Purslow.
   p. cm. -- (In the zone)
Includes index.
Summary: "Provides information about the fundamentals of rugby, from equipment and moves to superstars and legends. Intended for
third to fifth grade students"--Provided by publisher.
ISBN 978-1-62127-318-9 (hardcover : alk. paper) -- ISBN 978-1-62127-323-3 (softcover : alk. paper)
1. Rugby football--Juvenile literature. I. Title.
GV945.25.P87 2013
796.333--dc23

                    2012042225

Printed in the United States in North Mankato, Minnesota
1 2 3 4 5 6 7 8 9 0   17 16 15 14 13

012013
WEP301112

PROJECT COORDINATOR Aaron Carr
EDITOR Steve Macleod
ART DIRECTOR Terry Paulhus

CONTENTS

What Is **Rugby?**

The Rugby Union in England is made up of roughly 1,800 clubs and 2 million players.

In Rugby Union, players lift each other to try and catch the ball when it is thrown back into play after going out of bounds. This is called a lineout.

Rugby is played in more than 100 countries. Children and adults, both male and female, play rugby for fun. Some people also play for money. Running, passing, kicking, and tackling are all part of this **contact sport**. Speed, strength, and **stamina** are important skills for rugby players.

Rugby first began in the town of Rugby, England, in 1823. William Webb Ellis was a student at Rugby School and he became frustrated during a soccer game. He grabbed the ball with his hands, which is against the rules in soccer. Ellis carried the ball to the opponents' goal with the other team running close behind. A new sport was born.

Students continued to play rugby football. The game spread to other schools. In 1839, a team was established at the University of Cambridge in England. A set of rules for rugby was created at the same time. In 1871, a number of rugby teams came together in London to form the Rugby Football Union. Later that year, the first **international** rugby game was played between England and Scotland.

Some of the clubs in the Rugby Football Union disagreed on whether players should be paid for playing rugby. In 1895, 22 clubs left the Rugby Union and eventually created the Rugby League. Each organization has its own code, or set of rules. One of the big differences is the number of players on the field. Each team in a Rugby League game has two less players. The International Rugby Board (IRB) uses the code of the Rugby Union. These rules are used in more countries around the world than Rugby League, including the United States and Canada.

Rugby teams wear uniforms when they play. Players do not need a lot of equipment to play rugby. The most important piece of equipment needed to play rugby is a rugby ball.

Some players wear scrum caps to protect their ears. Other players wrap tape around the head to hold their ears flat instead.

Players wear shorts and long socks that match the colors of their team.

A rugby ball is oval and made of four panels. It is slightly rounder and larger than a football. The rugby ball is 11 to 12 inches (28 to 30 centimeters) long and 23 to 24 inches (58 to 62 cm) around the middle. The ball weighs between 14 and 16 ounces (410 and 460 grams).

■ Players wear a mouth guard to protect their teeth and help prevent **concussions**.

■ Rugby players wear jerseys with their number on the back. Jerseys are made of tough material so they do not rip easily. Some players also wear light shoulder padding under their uniforms.

■ Rugby jerseys have the team logo on the chest and the logo of team sponsors in other places on the uniform.

The Pitch

Rugby is played on a grass field called a pitch. It is a bit longer and wider than a football field. The pitches for both Rugby Union and Rugby League are 109 yards (100 meters) long. Rugby Union fields are 2 yards (2.5 m) wider than Rugby League fields.

There is a try zone at each end of the field. The try zone is sometimes called the in-goal area. White lines mark the boundaries of the pitch. Goalposts are set on the goal line at either end of the pitch. The goalposts are shaped like the letter "H." The posts are 18 feet (5.5 m) apart. There is a crossbar connecting them 10 feet (3 m) above the ground. The goalposts are usually covered with padding, so players will not be hurt if they run into them.

Rugby League

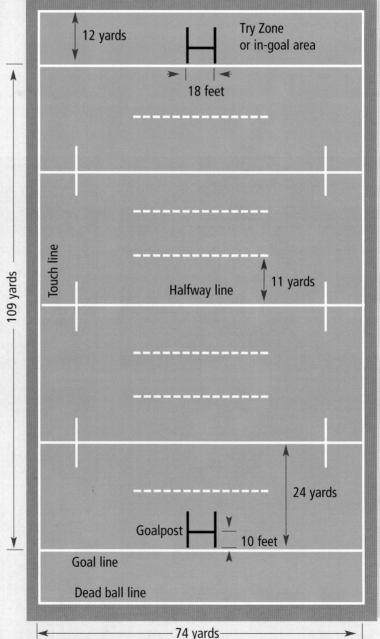

12 yards

Try Zone or in-goal area

18 feet

Touch line

109 yards

Halfway line

11 yards

24 yards

Goalpost

10 feet

Goal line

Dead ball line

74 yards

Rugby Union

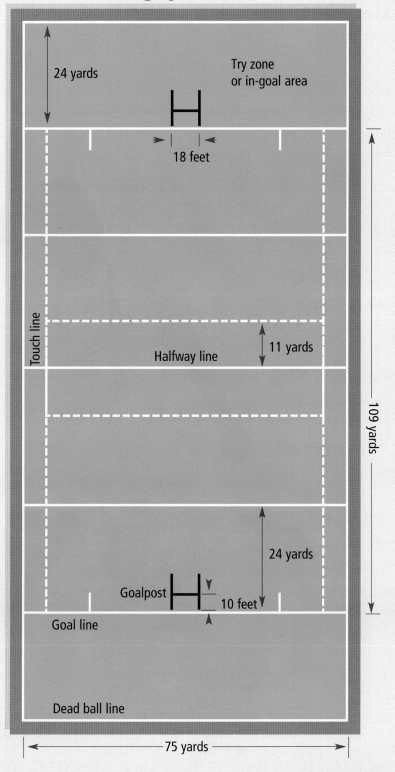

24 yards

Try zone
or in-goal area

18 feet

Touch line

Halfway line

11 yards

109 yards

24 yards

Goalpost

10 feet

Goal line

Dead ball line

75 yards

A rugby game is called a match. One referee and two judges oversee the match. It is played in two 40-minute halves with a 5 to 10 minute break at halftime. The teams switch ends after halftime.

A rugby ball cannot be passed forward. Players can carry it forward or kick it forward, but they can only pass it to teammates beside or behind them. The team with the most points after 80 minutes wins the match.

There are many ways to score points in rugby. Teams get the most points for scoring a try. This happens when the ball carrier runs across the goal line and touches the ball on the ground. A try is worth five points in Rugby Union and four points in Rugby League.

After a try is scored, a player on the team kicks the ball to gain more points for his or her team. Kickers can **place kick** or **drop kick** the ball as far out from the goal line as they want, but it must line up with where the ball was touched down in the try zone. If the ball goes through the goalposts, the team gains two points.

A penalty kick is worth three points in Rugby Union and two points in Rugby League.

At any time, any player can try to drop kick the ball through the goalposts. This means that for any of these kicks to be successful, they must pass between the goalposts and above the crossbar. The final way to score points is with a **penalty kick**. Referees can call penalties for many different **infractions**. When a team is awarded a penalty, the team captain can choose to kick for the goal or run with the ball.

If play is stopped due to an infraction, the forwards take part in a **scrum** to get the ball back in play. They link together by putting their arms around each other's shoulders. Then, they bend at the waist. At a signal from the referee, they engage, or **interlock**, with the forwards of the other team. Each group tries to overpower the other with its strength. The ball is rolled into the opening between the feet of the two groups. Each team tries to use their feet to hook the ball to a teammate outside of the scrum.

The scrum half rolls the ball into the scrum.

In Rugby Union, each team has 15 players on the field. There are eight forwards and seven backs. In Rugby League, each team has two less players on the field. There are six forwards and seven backs in Rugby League.

The number on a player's jersey is determined by the position they play on the field. In Rugby Union, the forwards wear numbers 1 to 8. In Rugby League, the forwards wear numbers 8 to 13.

Forwards are big, strong players that form the scrum. Three forwards are in the front row of the scrum. The middle forward is the hooker. It is the hooker's job to kick the ball back to his or her teammates.

The second row of forwards in the scrum supports the first row. They try to overpower the other team and get possession of the ball. When the ball rolls out of the scrum, the forwards pass the ball to the backs.

In Rugby Union, backs wear numbers 9 to 15. In Rugby League, the backs wear numbers 1 to 7.

The two forwards beside the hooker are called props. They help get the hooker in position to kick the ball back to their team.

The scrum half plays right behind the forwards. This player is the link between the forwards and the backs. It is similar to being the quarterback in football. When the ball comes out of the scrum, the scrum half decides which back is in the best position to receive the ball.

■ Most rugby passes are thrown underhand.

The backs then run the ball up the field. They can pass the ball to other backs who are running beside them or behind them. If a back is tackled to the ground by the other team, they must drop the ball. Players from each team surround the ball and form a ruck. A ruck is similar to a scrum. Players in a ruck try to push the other team backward so their backs can get the ball.

If a player with the ball is stopped but is not tackled to the ground a maul is formed. Each team surrounds the ball carrier and tries to gain possession of the ball using their arms and hands.

■ Running with two hands on the ball makes it easier for the player to either pass or kick the ball before being tackled.

Many boys and girls play rugby on community teams. Some of the leagues for younger players are non-contact. Players wear flags or are touched instead of tackled. When players are older they can play on high school, college, and university teams. They can also play for club teams. In North America, leagues have games and tournaments that are **endorsed** by USA Rugby and Rugby Canada.

Many cities in England have **professional** teams. Some cities in North America have professional teams as well. Professional players who play for these teams have the chance to be selected to play for their country's national team. When a player plays for his or her country in an international match, it is called a cap.

The three key international rugby tournaments are: the Rugby World Cup, Six Nations, and the Rugby Championship.

Twenty teams compete in the Rugby World Cup for the Webb Ellis Cup. The championship trophy is named after the boy who started the sport of rugby. New Zealand has won the Webb Ellis Cup two times.

The first Rugby World Cup was hosted by New Zealand and Australia in 1987. The tournament allows a country to establish itself as the world champion of rugby. The event takes place every four years. The U.S. national team is called the Eagles. The Eagles have played in five of the six Rugby World Cup competitions. The Women's Rugby World Cup also occurs every four years. It is held on different years than the men's event.

The countries involved in the Six Nations championship are England, Ireland, Scotland, Wales, France, and Italy. The tournament is played every year. It started in 1883 between England, Ireland, Scotland, and Wales. France joined in 1910, and Italy joined in 2000.

The Rugby Championship used to be called Tri Nations. It started in 1996 as a tournament between Australia, New Zealand, and South Africa. The New Zealand All Blacks have won the tournament 10 times. The name was changed to the Rugby Championship when Argentina joined the event in 2012.

Wales defeated France 16-9 to win the 2012 Six Nations championship.

Early Stars of Rugby

The sport of rugby has attracted many superb athletes. They thrill fans who fill the stands.

Serge Blanco

BORN: August 31, 1958
REPRESENTED: France
POSITION: Fullback

CAREER FACTS:

- He played for Les Bleus of France between 1980 and 1991. He represented France in international matches 93 times during those years.
- He was inducted into the International Rugby Hall of Fame in 1997 and the IRB Hall of Fame in 2011.
- Blanco was called the superman of rugby. He scored 233 points for France during his career.

Gareth Edwards

BORN: July 12, 1947
REPRESENTED: Wales
POSITION: Scrum Half

CAREER FACTS:

- He had 53 caps for Wales during his career between 1967 and 1978.
- Edwards earned 10 caps for the British Lions between 1968 and 1974.
- He was inducted into the International Rugby Hall of Fame in 1997.

Keith Wood

BORN: January 27, 1972
REPRESENTED: Ireland
POSITION: Hooker

CAREER FACTS:
- He had 58 caps for Ireland. He was captain of the team for 33 of those games. He also had 5 caps with the British Lions.
- Wood won the first ever IRB Player of the Year award in 2001.
- He was inducted into the International Rugby Hall of Fame in 2005.

John Eales

BORN: June 27, 1970
REPRESENTED: Australia
POSITION: Lock

CAREER FACTS:
- Eales is 6 feet 7 inches tall. He earned 86 caps as a forward for Australia and scored 173 points.
- He was named captain of the Australian team 55 times. His team won the World Cup in 1991 and 1999.
- Eales was inducted into the International Rugby Hall of Fame in 2005.

Superstars of Rugby

Rugby heroes of today have inspired
young athletes to try this exciting sport.

Jonny Wilkinson

BORN: May 25, 1979
REPRESENTED: England
POSITION: Fly Half

CAREER FACTS:

- Wilkinson scored a drop goal in the final seconds of the 2003 World Cup final. England beat Australia 20-17. He won the IRB International Player of the Year award that year.
- He has scored 1,179 points for the England national team.
- He was the third player in history to win the Golden Boot award for reaching 1,000 points in England's premier league.

Bryan Habana

BORN: June 12, 1983
REPRESENTED: South Africa
POSITION: Wing

CAREER FACTS:

- He won his first cap for South Africa in 2004. He scored a try the first time he touched the ball.
- Habana became South Africa's all-time leader in tries during the 2011 World Cup.

Richie McCaw

BORN: December 31, 1980
REPRESENTED: New Zealand
POSITION: Flanker

CAREER FACTS:
- McCaw was the first player to win the IRB International Player of the Year award more than once. He won it in 2006, 2009, and 2010.
- He led New Zealand to an 8-7 victory in the 2011 World Cup final versus France.
- McCaw set a record for most games as New Zealand captain, with 52 in 2010. He set a record in 2012 for most international wins by a player, with 94.

Todd Clever

BORN: January 16, 1983
REPRESENTED: United States
POSITION: Flanker

CAREER FACTS:
- He earned his first cap for the U.S. in 2003 versus Argentina.
- Clever has played professional rugby in the U.S., New Zealand, South Africa, and Japan. He is the current captain of the U.S. national team.
- Clever has earned 46 caps for the U.S. national team. He has scored 11 tries and 55 points for the Eagles.

A Healthy Player

There is a great deal of running in rugby, so players have to keep their bodies in good shape. They need to eat healthy foods and drink plenty of water. Eating balanced meals helps athletes work harder for longer periods of time.

The night before a match, many athletes eat **carbohydrates**, such as pasta, bread, and rice. The body stores this type of food as energy in the muscles and helps keep players from getting tired during a match.

■ Athletes need to drink fluids before, during, and after exercising.

■ Fruits and vegetables provide vitamins and minerals to keep athletes healthy.

Foods from the other food groups, such as fruits, vegetables, protein, and milk products, also have important **nutrients** needed for a healthy body. Strong bones and muscles are important when playing a sport that requires speed and strength.

Athletes need to drink water to replace what they lose when they sweat. When muscles work hard, they produce heat in the body. To keep cool, the body releases heat through sweat.

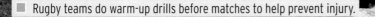
Rugby teams do warm-up drills before matches to help prevent injury.

Rugby Brain Teasers

Test your rugby knowledge by trying to answer these brain teasers!

1 Which player picks the ball up from the scrum?

2 Why do rugby players wear mouth guards?

3 What is the name of the trophy handed out to the winner of the rugby World Cup?

4 What four countries compete in the Rugby Championship?

5 What do rugby players call the field they play on?

6 How many points is a try worth?

ANSWERS: 1. The scrum half. 2. Players wear mouth guards to protect their teeth and help prevent concussions. 3. The Webb Ellis Cup. 4. The four countries are Argentina, Australia, New Zealand, and South Africa. 5. It is called the pitch. 6. A try is worth five points in Rugby Union and four points in Rugby League.

Key Words

carbohydrates: foods that provide energy

concussions: injuries to the brain from being hit on the head

contact sport: a sport where physical contact is allowed

drop kick: a kick when the ball is dropped from the player's hands

endorsed: supported

infraction: an error or a broken rule

interlock: connect two or more things together

international: involving two or more countries

nutrients: substances needed by the body and obtained from food

penalty kick: a place kick that occurs after a penalty is called and the kicker thinks he is within range to score

place kick: a kick in which the ball is placed on a plastic tee on the ground

professional: an athlete who earns money for playing a sport

scrum: when the forwards on each team come together and try to gain possession of the ball

stamina: the ability to do something for a long time

Index

Log on to www.av2books.com

AV² by Weigl brings you media enhanced books that support active learning. Go to www.av2books.com, and enter the special code found on page 2 of this book. You will gain access to enriched and enhanced content that supplements and complements this book. Content includes video, audio, weblinks, quizzes, a slide show, and activities.

AV² Online Navigation

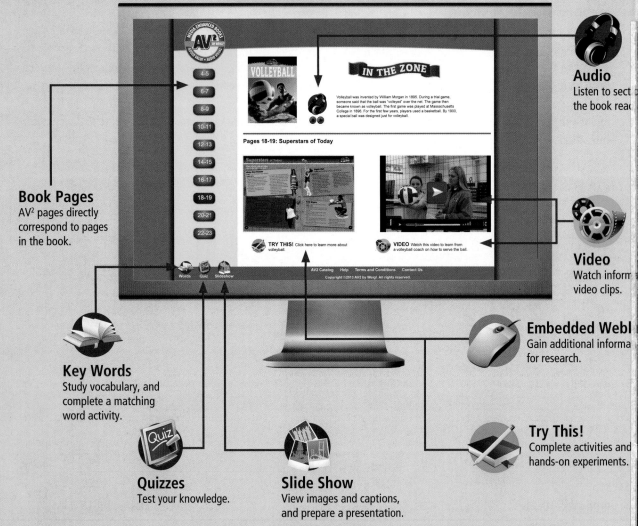

Audio
Listen to sect
the book read

Book Pages
AV² pages directly correspond to pages in the book.

Video
Watch inform
video clips.

Embedded Webl
Gain additional informa
for research.

Key Words
Study vocabulary, and complete a matching word activity.

Try This!
Complete activities and
hands-on experiments.

Quizzes
Test your knowledge.

Slide Show
View images and captions, and prepare a presentation.

AV² was built to bridge the gap between print and digital. We encourage you to tell us what you like and what you want to see in the future.

Sign up to be an AV² Ambassador at www.av2books.com/ambassador.

Due to the dynamic nature of the Internet, some of the URLs and activities provided as part of AV² by Weigl may have changed or ceased to exist. AV² by Weigl accepts no responsibility for any such changes. All media enhanced books are regularly monitored to update addresses and sites in a timely manner. Contact AV² by Weigl at 1-866-649-3445 or av2books@weigl.com with any questions, comments, or feedback.